For Dave

Library of Congress Cataloging-in-Publication Data
Seibert, Patricia.
Discovering El Niño: how fable and fact together
help explain the weather / by Patricia Seibert;
illustrated by Jan Davey Ellis.
p. cm.
Summary: Traces the weather phenomenon known as El Niño
from its first observation near Peruvian fishing villages to
more recent appearances, discussing how scientists monitor it
and how it affects other aspects of the weather.
ISBN 0-7613-1273-0 (lib. bdg.)
1. El Niño Current—Juvenile literature. 2. Climatic changes—Juvenile
literature. [1. El Niño Current.] I. Ellis, Jan Davey, ill. II. Title.
GC296.8.E4S45 1999
551.5'24642—dc21 99-13757 CIP

Published by The Millbrook Press, Inc.
2 Old New Milford Road
Brookfield, Connecticut 06804
Visit our Web site: http://www.millbrookpress.com

DISCOVERING EL NIÑO

How Fable and Fact Together
Help Explain the Weather

By Patricia Seibert

Illustrated by Jan Davey Ellis

The Millbrook Press   Brookfield, Connecticut

Fishermen live and die by the weather. If the weather conditions are right, there are many fish to be caught. If the weather conditions are wrong, there will be few or no fish when the fishermen cast their nets.

All around the world, fishermen look at the sky, feel the wind, and examine the water. They think, *Is today a good day? Where are the fish swimming today? Where should I drop my nets to catch the most fish?*

Hundreds of years ago, fishermen had the same thoughts. Today, fishermen who sail on the oceans have fancier boats and more complicated equipment than fishermen of the distant past. In spite of all this, Mother Nature still controls the conditions that mean good fishing or bad fishing.

The country of Peru is in South America, just south of the equator. (The equator is an imaginary line around the middle of the Earth. The half of the Earth above the equator is called the Northern Hemisphere, and the half below the equator is the Southern Hemisphere.) Peru is bordered on the west by the Pacific Ocean.

SOUTH AMERICA

EQUATOR

Peru

Pacific
Ocean

Atlantic
Ocean

For centuries Peruvian fishermen set off in their boats and traveled along the ocean coast. They cast their nets and then drew them back up, full of fish. Over time, the fishermen grew very wise about the ways of the sea. They noticed that each year there was a period of time when their fishing waters would grow warmer. The fishermen observed that the normal ocean current, which usually flowed from the south up to the north, would flow in the opposite direction. The changed current seemed to bring in warmer waters along the coast.

Some years when the change in current came, the water along the coast of Peru would become so warm that the fish had trouble living in it. One important reason was that the fish had trouble finding enough food.

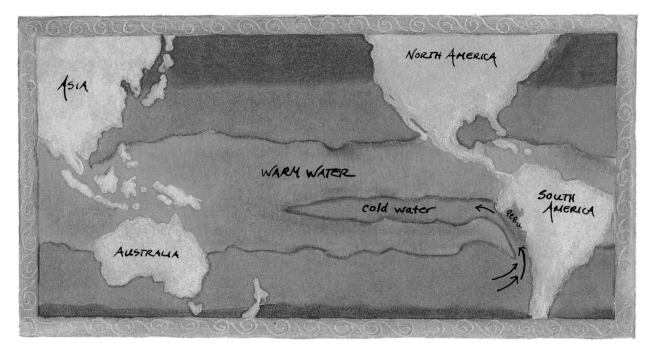

NORMAL OCEAN
CURRENTS

COLD
WATER

WARM
WATER

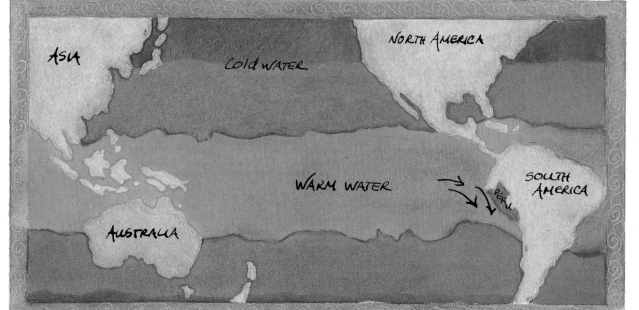

EL NIÑO
OCEAN CURRENTS

Most of the time, the coastal waters were full of sea life—animals and plants—that the fish liked to eat. During the years that the ocean waters increased in temperature quite a lot instead of just a little, many plants could not adjust well to the change and just died off.

With the food supply gone, most of the fish would move, or migrate, to a new location where the water was cooler. However, the Peruvian fishermen had houses and families in villages along the seacoast and could not sail far enough or fish deep enough to find cooler waters where the fish were plentiful. The fishermen suffered through the time of empty nets, waiting for the cooler waters to return.

The seabirds suffered, too. Without fish to eat, the birds starved. In bad years many birds would die, and many of their bodies would fall into the sea. The decaying bodies of the seabirds created a chemical compound called hydrogen sulfide. The hydrogen sulfide and the salty water of the ocean combined to make a very strong acid, which could eat through the paint on the hulls of boats. The wind carried this acid through the air to the houses along the shore, discoloring their paint. The fishermen called this effect "the Callao painter." Callao is the name of a city on the Pacific coast of Peru.

Another effect of the dead birds was that there were no more of their droppings along the beaches. The bird droppings, called "guano," made good fertilizer. Some Peruvian villagers made their living gathering the guano to sell. No bird droppings meant trouble for the guano gatherers.

In the years when there was a dramatic change in sea temperature, a chain reaction was started. There were not as many sea creatures and plants for the fish to eat, so the fish moved to find waters with more food. No fish meant that the birds starved to death. The dead birds were, of course, leaving no droppings, so guano gatherers had less to sell. Also, the bodies of the birds were decaying in the sea, which created a chemical compound that discolored paint on boats and houses. It is easy to understand why some people who lived along the Peruvian coast hundreds of years ago would keep journal records about the times when the ocean waters would turn especially warm.

In fact, historians and scientists have found personal journals and logs from ships, some as old as five hundred years, that have descriptions of what happened when the ocean water turned warm. Reading about what happened in the past helped scientists uncover patterns in the weather—events that happen again and again, in the same way or at the same time of year.

NO FISH IN WARMER WATER ...

DEAD BIRDS..... NO GUANO....

RE-PAINTING BOAT

WRITING IN JOURNAL

Before any scientific studies were ever published, the fishermen were passing along stories about the patterns of the weather and the sea. Many of the fishermen in Peru were followers of the Christian religion. They realized that the warmer waters would arrive each year close to the Christmas holiday, when they were celebrating the birth of the Christ child.

Since the fishermen spoke Spanish, they called the Christ child "El Niño." In Spanish, the term *el niño* means "little one" or "little boy." When the term is spelled with capital letters (El Niño), it is used to refer to the baby Jesus. Since the warm current came each year around Christmastime, the fishermen named the current El Niño.

In the late 1800s a Peruvian scientist wrote a short article about the warm ocean current that sometimes occurred off the coast of Peru. The scientist told how the fishermen used the name El Niño for the warm current. He also noted that in some years, when there were especially strong effects from El Niño, much rain was falling in places that were usually dry.

As the years passed, scientists in South America continued to gather information about El Niño. In addition, scientists from all over the world were studying the oceans and the weather, trying to better understand them.

Early in the 1900s, Sir Gilbert Walker, a scientist from Great Britain, was studying the monsoons in India. Monsoons are terrifically strong winds that blow from the northeast to bring in cool dry weather in winter, but then shift around to the southwest in summer to bring in warm, extremely wet weather. Thus, monsoons have a powerful influence on the weather in India.

As Walker tried to understand monsoons better, and perhaps learn how to predict when they would come and how strong their effects might be, he looked at records of weather from all around the world. His studies led him to believe that there were connections between the weather happening on one part of the Earth and events happening on the other side of the planet. However, Sir Gilbert could not gather enough information to prove his idea, so that many people did not believe what he had found. For example, Canada or the United States seemed too far away to be affected by the weather in India.

Sir Gilbert spent time studying the changes in air pressure on the east and west sides of the Pacific Ocean. Meanwhile, other scientists were keeping similar records. As Walker studied these records, he realized that whenever the pressure was high on the eastern side of the Pacific, it was low on the western side. And when the air pressure was low in the east, it was high in the west.

Sir Gilbert named this condition in the atmosphere the Southern Oscillation since the air pressure changes take place in the Southern Hemisphere—the half of the Earth south of the equator. Oscillation means movement back and forth or up and down with regularity.

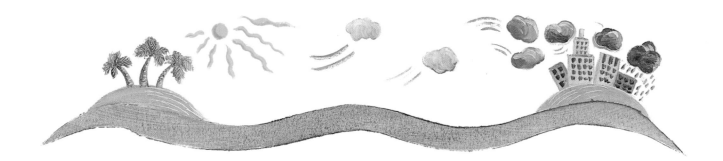

It took fifty years before scientists were able to make a connection between the Southern Oscillation, named by Sir Gilbert, and El Niño, the warm sea current named by Peruvian fishermen. A scientist from Norway, Jacob Bjerknes, who was working at a university in the United States, noticed something important as he studied all kinds of scientific data about the weather. He saw that whenever the temperature of the ocean off the coast of Peru was quite warm (a strong El Niño), the easterly winds blowing over the ocean from South America west toward Australia would be quite weak. In addition, during the years that the temperatures at the surface of the ocean were not much warmer than usual (a weak El Niño), then the easterly winds were blowing strongly.

So, after years of observation and study by scientists from all over the world, enough information had been collected for scientists to decide that El Niño and the Southern Oscillation were part of the same huge weather pattern. Some scientists began calling the huge weather pattern ENSO (El Niño-Southern Oscillation).

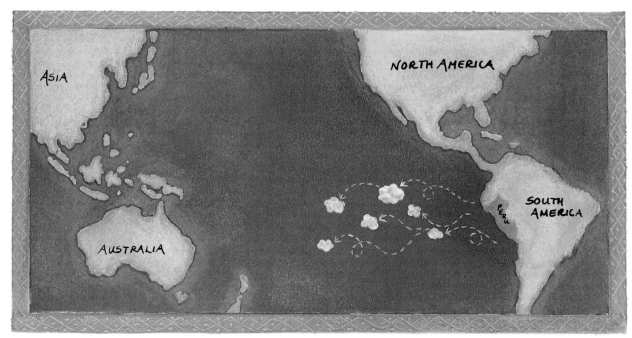

← Warm water

← weak winds

← STRONG EL NIÑO
YEAR

← cold water

← Strong winds

← weak EL NIÑO
YEAR

Scientists continued to collect facts, and to think about what they were learning. They realized that warmer ocean waters had a big influence on where large thunderstorms developed. The large thunderstorms were so powerful that they influenced how the air circulated in the skies. Air circulation affects how and where winds blow around the world. The winds carry warm air, cool air, moist air, or dry air to different parts of the Earth, and help create the weather that different parts of the world experience.

El Niño can spread its effects around the world by changing the location where ocean waters are warmest. Where ocean waters are warmest is where these powerful thunderstorms will be created. Thus, the location of the thunderstorms influences how the wind blows and affects the weather all over the world in different ways.

During the many years that fishermen, and later scientists, have watched and talked about El Niño, the name has meant different things to different people. The fishermen who first used the name thought of El Niño as the warm ocean current that arrived every year around the Christmas holiday. Now, when people talk about El Niño, they usually mean the current only in those years that it is warm enough to affect conditions off the coast of Peru—and perhaps affect weather in other parts of the world. Some people also use the term El Niño to mean the giant ENSO weather pattern.

Some scientists say El Niño comes every three to seven years, some say every two to seven. There is much information to be studied, so there is not complete agreement on which years have enough changes to be classified as El Niño years.

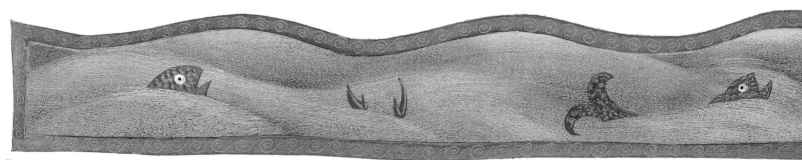

During a weak El Niño year, the warm current usually does not last much longer than a month. In a strong year, El Niño can hang around for several months—even longer than a year in some cases. Scientists do not always agree about how long a particular El Niño has lasted. In the last forty years, there have been about ten events in which El Niño was strong enough to cause a warm episode—that is, warm enough to have quite a few effects that were felt over a large area.

Sometimes the opposite of El Niño happens where the temperatures on the surface of the ocean off the coast of Peru are cooler than normal. Many scientists have started using the name "La Niña" to refer to this cold phase. La Niña years happen about half as often as El Niño years.

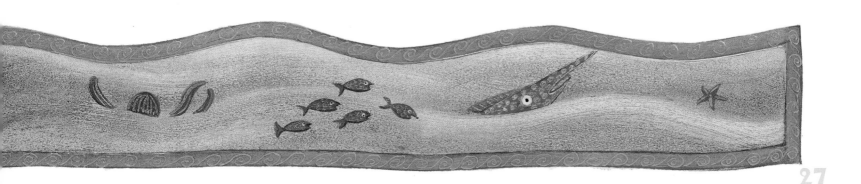

The years in between El Niño years and La Niña years can be thought of as the average years. But it is easy to see that change is normal since the conditions in the seas and the skies are constantly changing. Scientists continue to gather as much information as they can, so that they can find patterns in the changes. Then scientists can predict more accurately what is going to happen and when. Accurate predictions can help people make plans to protect themselves and their property from severe weather.

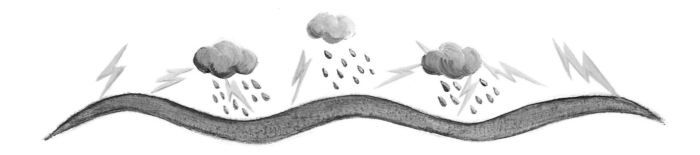

Even so, just as the fishermen in Peru long ago had little choice but
to wait for the fish to return, people around the world sometimes
have little choice in the face of Mother Nature's power. Nevertheless,
learning about the phenomenon that is called El Niño is important
and helpful. When it comes to dealing with the weather and its effects
on people all around the world, the best—and often the only—
strategy is to study and learn as much as possible.

More Information About The Kinds of Effects That a Powerful El Niño Can Have

In the years when El Niño is powerful, it can have many effects. Some of the effects are good for people and animals, but some are terrible.

Not all scientists agree on which events are caused by a strong El Niño weather pattern. Often, conditions in the atmosphere have many different causes. However, a strong El Niño does seem to be connected to a wide variety of changes in the weather. This is why more and more scientists are trying to learn as much as possible about El Niño.

Here are some of the events that have occurred during El Niño years:

Both floods and droughts can happen during a year when El Niño is strong. Since an El Niño can cause shifts in patterns of rainfall—where the rain falls and how much rain falls— much more rain than usual can fall in one area, causing flooding. People's houses may be washed away. Not enough rain falls in other areas, so droughts occur. Then food crops die, and there might not be enough food for people who live in the area. There might not even be enough water for drinking or washing. So sometimes people can really suffer because of the impact of an El Niño.

Sea lions and seals that live off the west coast of the United States die in larger numbers than usual when there is not enough food. The changes that are brought by an El Niño can result in warmer waters where the seals and sea lions live. This pushes many fish and squid—the main food supply of seals and sea lions—to cooler waters at other locations. For the most part, the seals and sea lions stay put, so many of them starve to death.

During some years lots of snow falls in the mountains in California and Nevada. Sometimes those big snowfalls are said to be the result of weather conditions created by an El Niño. All the snow is great for skiers. In the spring the melting snow produces water that farmers need and would otherwise have to pump up from wells. Skiers, ski resort owners, and farmers really like the snows that can result from an El Niño.

Bananas can develop a fungus. Ecuador, a country right next to Peru, is a place where many bananas are grown. An El Niño can cause heavy rains during the season when banana-growing areas are usually sunny and dry. Then, not as many bananas grow successfully. And the wet conditions mean the bananas can get a fungal disease called "black sigatoka," which causes bananas to ripen more quickly than usual. This is a big problem for the portion of the banana crop that needs to be shipped to faraway countries.

Usually, only a modest number of wildflowers bloom in the desert areas in the southern part of California and along the coastal areas of Peru. But if an El Niño creates conditions that cause increased rainfall, then those desert regions can be covered with wide areas of colorful wildflowers.

Sometimes bug populations increase in the United States in years when an El Niño helps create conditions that are favorable to certain insects. When the winters are mild, more bugs may be able to survive. But bugs can be helped or hurt by many different factors, so most scientists do not think it makes sense to connect an El Niño too closely with more bugs or fewer bugs.